POPULAR 101 SONGS

EASY SHEET MUSIC

FOR KIDS

TROMBONE

WITH SIMPLE CHORDS

TEDDY CLARK

Chase

Traditional

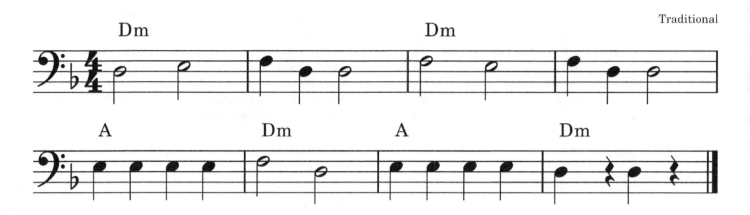

Hot Cross Buns

Traditional

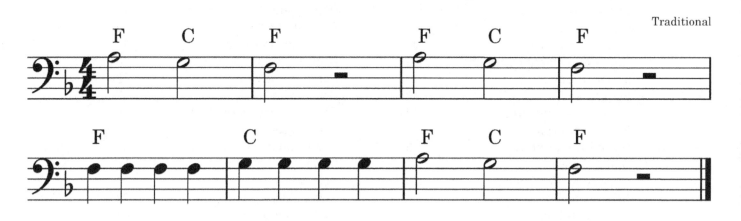

Au Clair de la Lune

French Traditional

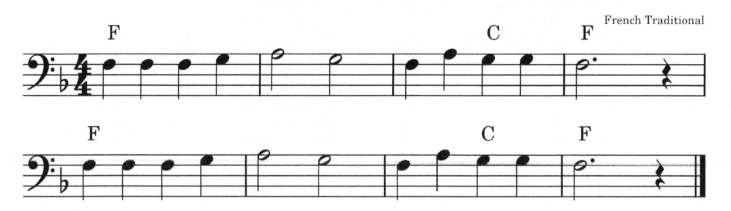

Mary Had a Little Lamb

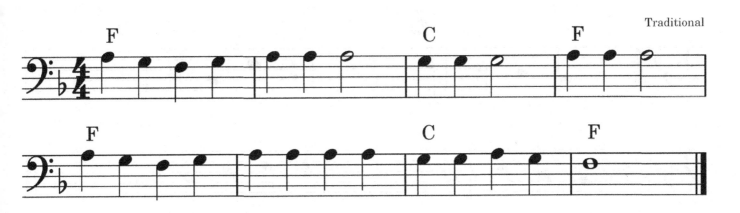

Good King Wenceslas

Go Tell Aunt Rhody

Jumping Heart

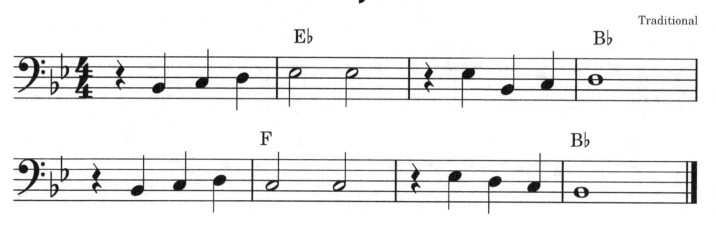

Oats and Beans

Aura Lee

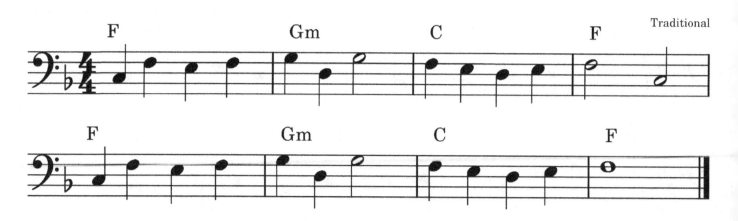

God Is So Good

Traditional

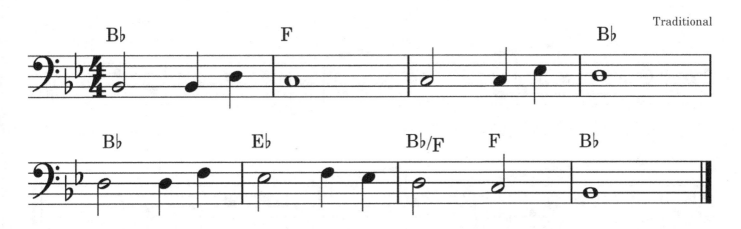

Largo

Antonin Dvorak

Rondo Alla Turca

Wolfgang Amadeus Mozart

Musette

Johann Sebastian Bach

The Banks Of The Ohio

Traditional

8

Morning Mood

Edvard Grieg

When the Saints

Traditional

9

Twinkle Twinkle Little Star

Wolfgang Amadeus Mozart

Pop! Goes the Weasel

Traditional

London Bridge

Traditional English Song

Jingle Bells

Traditional Christmas Song

Are You Sleeping?

French Folk Song

Lightly Row

Traditional

This Old Man

Traditional

Long, Long Ago

Thomas Bayly

13

Rock My Soul

African-American Spiritual

Oh! Susanna

Stephen Foster

Trumpet Concerto

Joseph Haydn

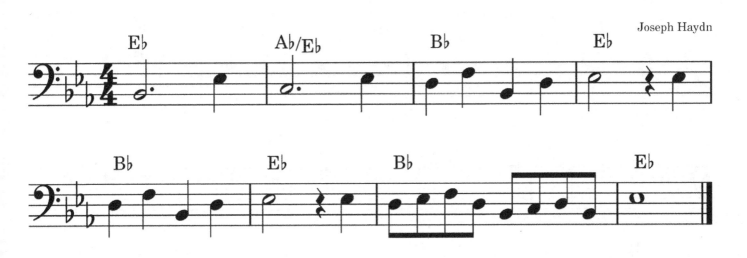

Old McDonald

Traditional

Chopsticks

Euphemia Allen

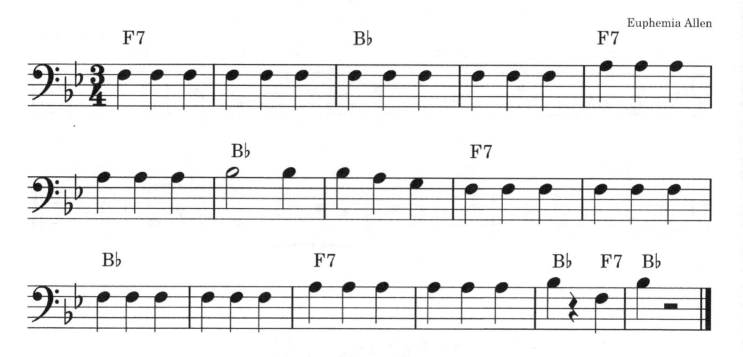

Itsy Bitsy Spider

Traditional Danish

Alouette

Traditional

Ode to Joy

Ludwig van Beethoven

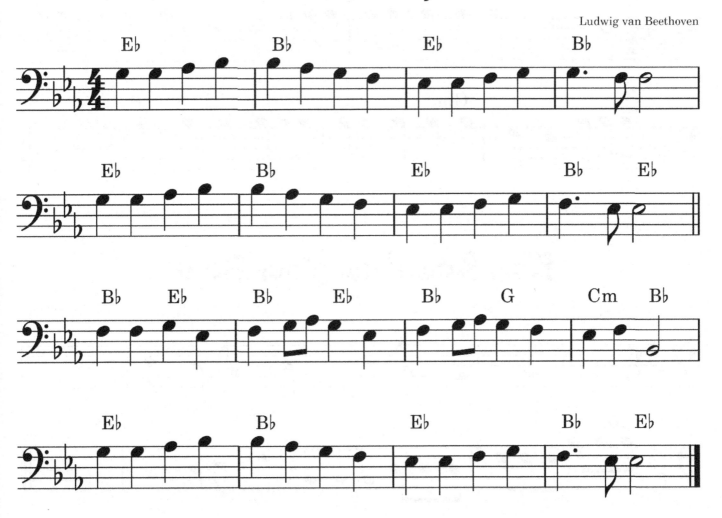

Yankee Doodle

American Traditional

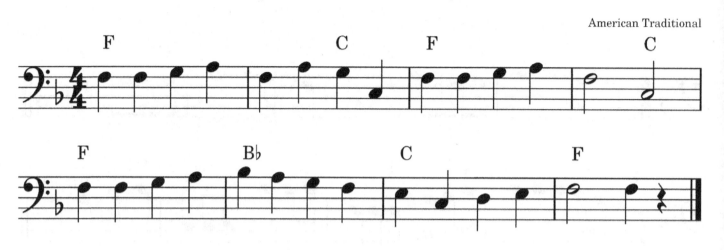

Baby Shark

Traditional

Row Row Row Your Boat

Traditional

The Muffin Man

English Rhyme

Holy, Holy, Holy

John Bacchus Dykes

Carnival of Venice

Julius Benedict

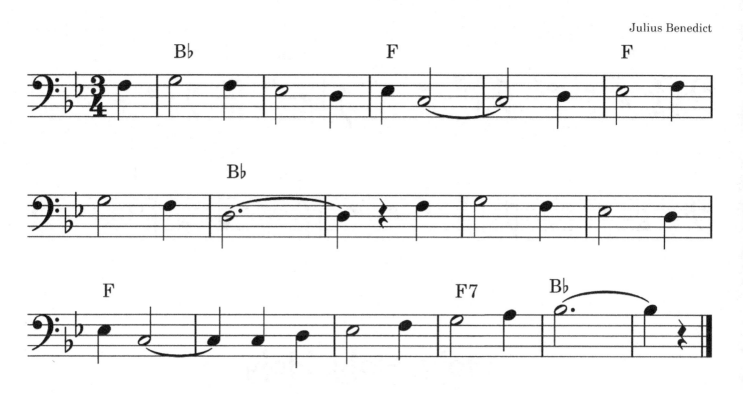

Pat-A-Cake

Traditional

Bingo

Traditional

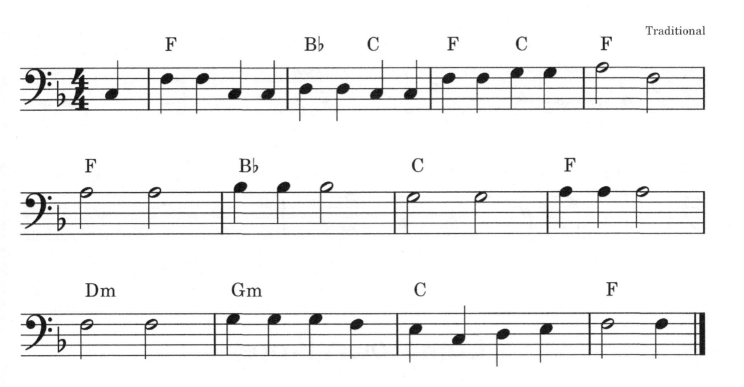

Mexican Hat Dance

Traditional

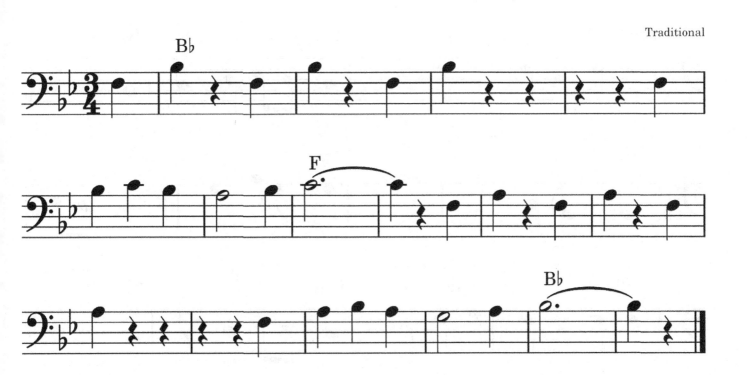

21

Happy Birthday

Traditional

Camptown Races

Stephen Foster

One Potato Two Potatoes

Nursery rhyme

Swan Lake

Pyotr Ilyich Tchaikovsky

Lavender's Blue

English folk song

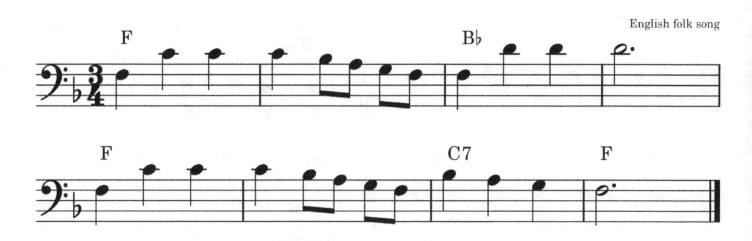

Beautiful Minka

Ludwig van Beethoven

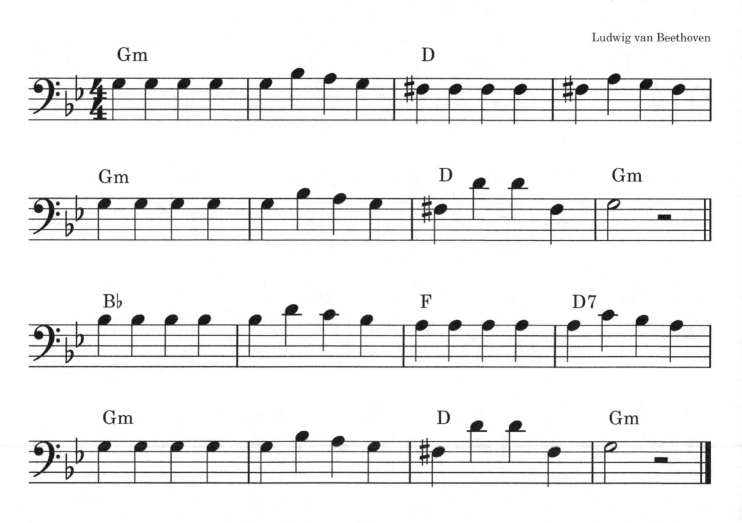

Air

Wolfgang. A. Mozart

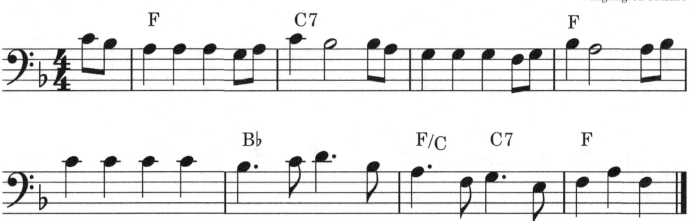

Joy to the World

George F. Handel

25

Humpty Dumpty

Mother Goose nursery rhyme

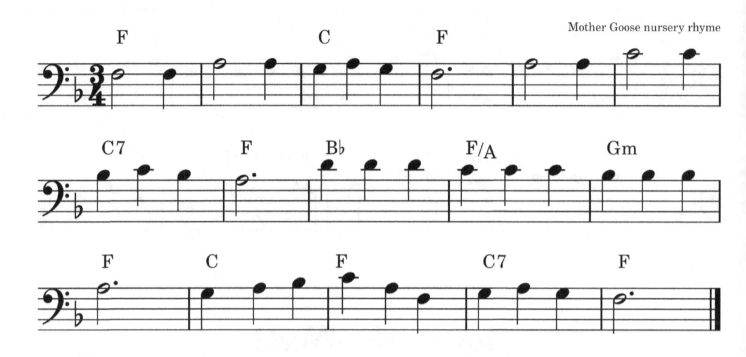

Kum Ba Yah

Traditional

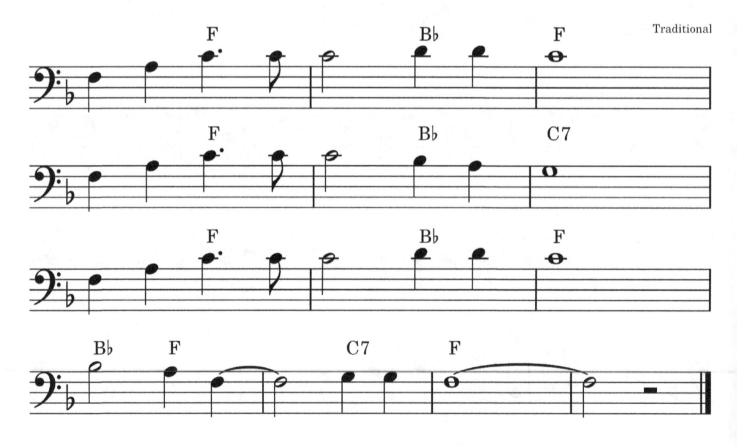

Amazing Grace

John Newton

Hava Nagila

Hebrew Folksong

Bella Ciao

Italian Traditional

Auld Lang Syne

Scottish Folksong

Deck the Halls

Traditional

Up on the Housetop

Benjamin Hanby

Wellerman

Sea Shanty

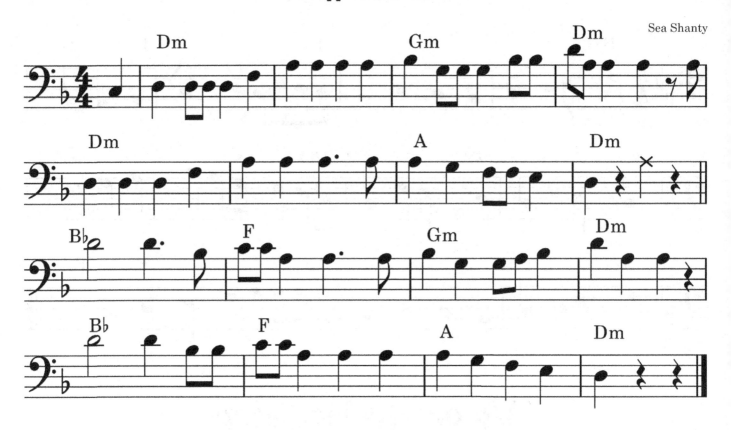

Drunken Sailor

Sea Shanty

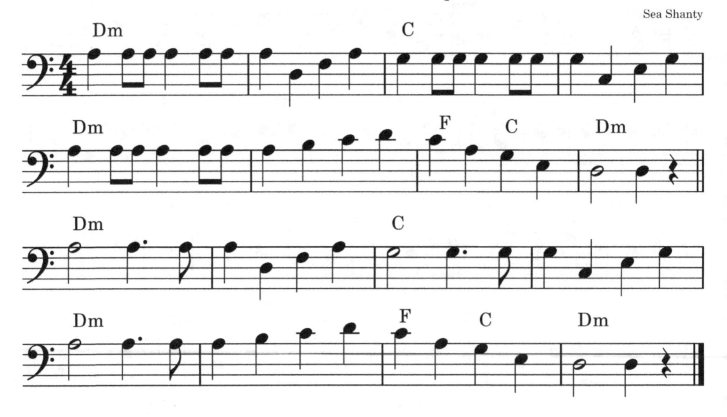

Ding Dong Merrily on High

Jehan Tabourot

Angels We Have Heard On High

French carol

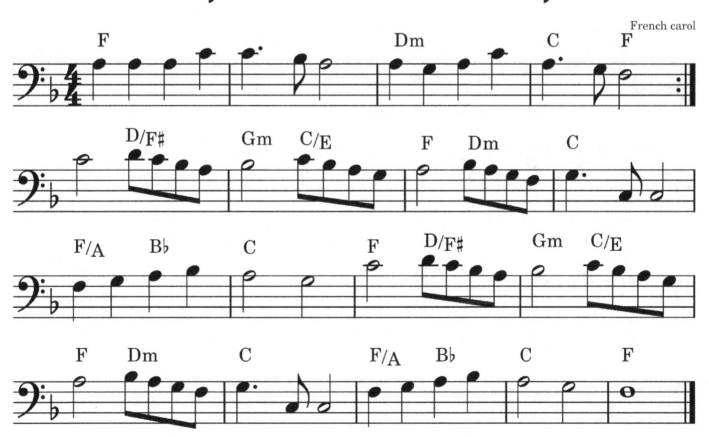

Symphony No. 7

Ludwig van Beethoven

Romance de Amour

Anonymous

Scarborough Fair

Traditional English

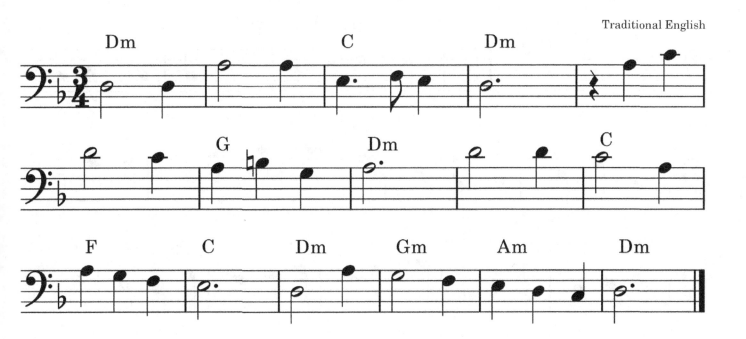

Can Can

Jacques Offenbach

Away in a Manger

W. J. Kirkpatrick

O Christmas Tree

Melchior Franck

We Wish You a Merry Christmas

Traditional

O Come, All Ye Faithful

Traditional

The First Noel

Traditional English Carol

William Tell Overture

Gioachino Rossini

Hallelujah Chorus

Georg Friedrich Handel

Barcarolle

Jacques Offenbach

Home on the Range

Traditional

Spring

Antonio Vivaldi

Moonlight Sonata

Ludwig van Beethoven

Kalinka

Russian Folk Song

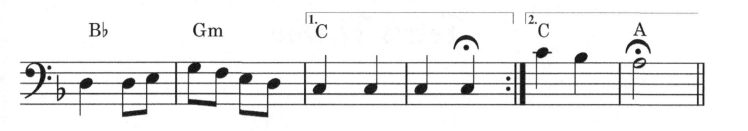

Tetris Theme

Russian Folk Song

Symphony No. 6

Ludwig van Beethoven

Wedding March

Felix Mendelssohn-Bartholdy

Bridal Chorus

Richard Wagner

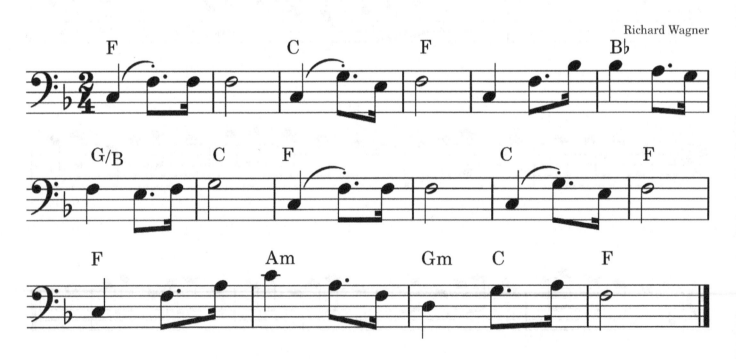

Water Music

Georg F. Handel

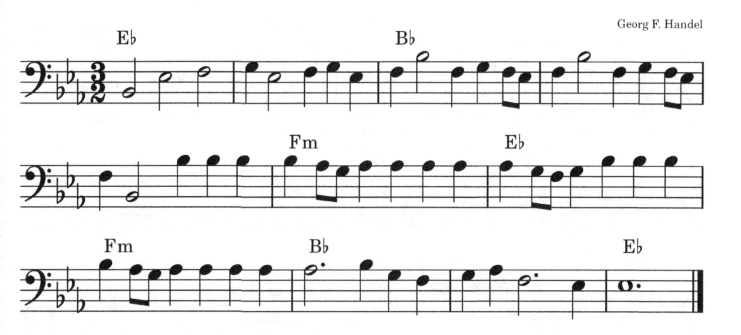

Liebestraum

Franz Lisz

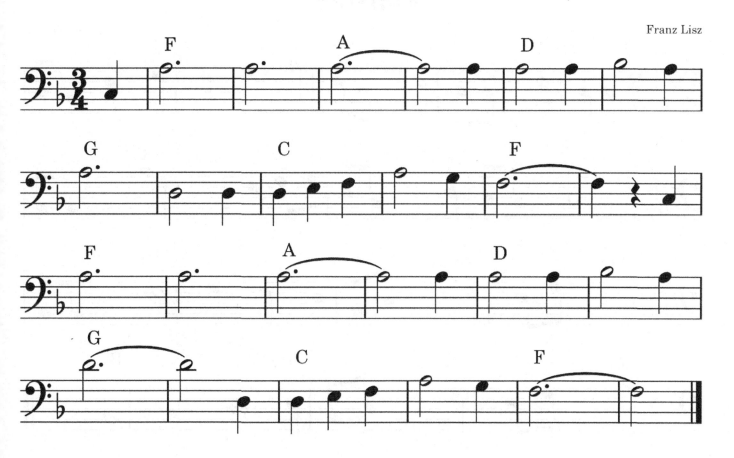

La Donna e Mobile

Giuseppe Verdi

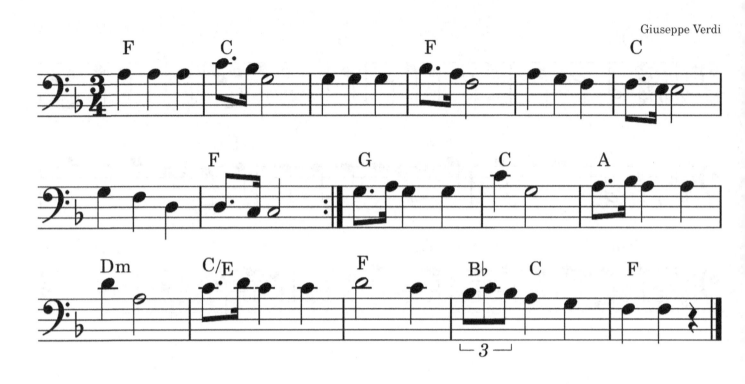

Lullaby

Johannes Brahms

Canon in D

Johann Pachelbel

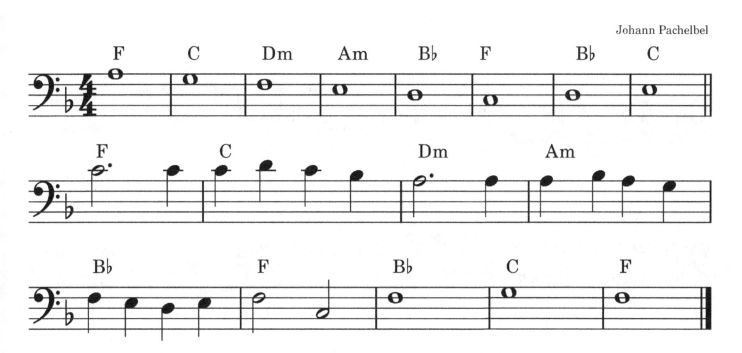

Summertime

George Gershwin

Glory Glory Hallelujah!

Julia Ward Howe

52

Silent Night

Franz Gruber

La Cumparsita

G. H. Matos Rodriguez

La Cucaracha

Mexian Folk Song

March of the Toreadors

Georges Bizet

56

Hungarian Dance No. 5

Johannes Brahms

Danse Macabre

Camille Saint-Saëns

58

Greensleeves

English Folk Song

Jesu, Joy of Man's Desiring

Johann Sebastian Bach

Ecossaise

Ludwig van Beethoven

Eine Kleine Nachtmusik

Wolfgang Amadeus Mozart

O Holy Night

Adolphe Charles Adam

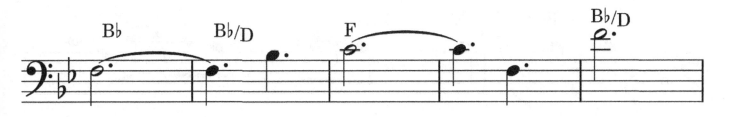

The Entertainer

Scott Joplin

66

Nutcracker March

Peter Ilyich Tchaikovsky

Air
Wolfgang Amadeus Mozart, 1756-1791

Alouette
French folk song

Amazing Grace
Words: John Newton (1725–1807)
Music: Tune of *New Britain,* ca. 19th century

Angels We Have Heard on High
Words: French carol, ca. 1862
Music: French carol

Are You Sleeping?
Traditional French song

Au Clair de la Lune
French folk song of the 18th century

Auld Lang Syne
Words: Robert Burns, 1788
Music: Scots folk

Aura Lee
Words: William Whiteman Fosdick, 1825-1862
Music: George R. Poulton, 1828-1867

Away in a Manger
Words: Anon., ca. 1882, Philadelphia
Music: "Cradle Song" by William J. Kirkpatrick

Baby Shark
Traditional nursery rhyme, ca. 20th century

Barcarolle
Music: Jacques Offenbach, 1819-1880

Beautiful Minka
Russian folk song
Ludwig van Beethoven, 1770-1827

Bella Ciao
Italian protest folk song, 19th century

Bingo
Roud folk song, 1780

Bridal Chorus
Richard Wagner, 1813-1883

Camptown Races
Words and music: Stephen Foster, 1850

Can Can
Music: Jacques Offenbach, 1819-1880

Canon in D
Johann Pachelbel, 1653- 1706

Carnival of Venice
Traditional Italian
Music: tune of "O Mamma, Mamma Cara"

Chase
Music: unknown

Chopsticks
Euphemia Allen, 1877

Danse Macabre
Charles Camille Saint-Saëns, 1835-1921

Deck the Halls
Words: Thomas Oliphant, ca. 1862
Music: Welsh traditional, ca. 16th century

Ding Dong Merrily on High
Words: George Ratcliffe Woodward, 1848–1934
Music: Jehan Tabourot, 1519-1593

Drunken Sailor
Sea shanty, ca. 19th century

Ecossaise
Ludwig van Beethoven, 1770-1827

Eine Kleine Nachtmusik
Wolfgang Amadeus Mozart, 1756-1791

Glory Glory Hallelujah!
Words: Julia Ward Howe, 1819-1910
Music: William Steffe, 1830-1890

Go Tell Aunt Rhody
Words: English folk song, ca. 19th century
Music: Jeana-Jacquesa Rousseau, 1712-1778

God Is So Good
Words & Music: Traditional

Good King Wenceslas
Words: John Mason Neale, ca. 1853
Music: tune of "Eastertime Has Come", 13th century

Greensleeves
Traditional English, 16th century

Hallelujah Chorus
Music: Georg Friedrich Handel, 1685-1759

Hallelujah Chorus
Music: Georg Friedrich Handel, 1685-1759

Happy Birthday
Words and music: Patty Hill, Mildred J. Hill, 1893

Hava Nagila
Jewish folk song, 1918

Holy, Holy, Holy
Words: Reginald Heber, 1783–1826
Tune of "Nicaea", John Bacchus Dykes, 1823-1876

Home on the Range
Words: Brewster M. Higley, 1823-1911
Music: Daniel E. Kelley, 1808-1905

Hot Cross Buns
Traditional

Humpty Dumpty
Mother Goose nursery rhyme

Hungarian Dance No 5
Johannes Brahms, 1833-1897

Itsy Bitsy Spider
Traditional Danish

Jesu, Joy of Man's Desiring
Johann Sebastian Bach, 1685-1750

Jingle Bells
Words and music: James Lord Pierpont, ca. 1850

Joy to the World
Words: Isaac Watts, 1674-1748
Music: George F. Handel, 1685-1759

Jumping Heart
Traditional

Kalinka
Words and music: Ivan Larionov, 1860

Kum Ba Yah
African American Spiritual

La Cucaracha
Mexican folk song

La Cumparsita
Gerardo Hernán Matos Rodríguez, 1916

La Donna e Mobile
Giuseppe Verdi, 1813-1901

Largo
Antonin Dvorak, 1841-1904

Lavender's Blue
English nursery rhyme, 17th century

Liebestraum
Franz Liszt, 1811-1886

Lightly Row
Words: Franz Wiedemann, 1821–1882
Music: German folk song

London Bridge
Traditional English, ca. 1744

Long, Long Ago
Words and music: Thomas Haynes Bayly, 1833

Lullaby
Johannes Brahms, 1833-1897

March of the Toreadors
Georges Bizet, 1838-1875

Mary Had a Little Lamb
Words: Sarah Josepha Hale, 1788-1879
Music: Traditional nursery song

Mexican Hat Dance
Traditional

Moonlight Sonata
Ludwig van Beethoven, 1770-1827

Morning Mood
Edvard Grieg, 1843-1907

Musette
Johann Sebastian Bach, 1685-1750

Nutcracker March
Peter Ilyich Tchaikovsky, 1840-1893

O Christmas Tree
Words: Ernst Anschutz, ca. 1824
Music: Melchior Franck, ca. 16th Century

O Come All Ye Faithful
Words and music: John F. Wade, ca. 1711-1786

O Holy Night
Words: John Sullivan Dwight, 1813–1893
Music: Adolphe Charles Adam, 1803-1856

Oats and Beans
Traditional British and American folk song

Ode to Joy
Words: Henry van Dyke, 1907
Music: Ludwig van Beethoven, 1770-1827

Oh When the Saints
Traditional gospel hymn

Oh! Susanna
Words and music: Stephen Foster, 1848

Old McDonald
Music: Thomas D'Urfey, 1706
Traditional children's song

One Potato Two Potatoes
Nursery rhyme, 1885
Music: unknown

Pat-A-Cake
Traditional, 1698
Music: unknown

Pop! Goes the Weasel
English nursery rhyme, 18th century

Rock My Soul
Traditional African American spiritual
Romance de Amour
Music: unknown, 19th century

Rondo Alla Turca
Wolfgang Amadeus Mozart, 1756-1791

Row Row Row Your Boat
Popular children's song, 1852

Scarborough Fair
Traditional English ballad, 16th century

Silent Night
Words: Joseph Mohr, 1792-1848
Music: Franz Gruber, 1787-1863

Spring
Antonio Vivaldi, 1678-1741

Summertime
George Gershwin, 1898-1937

Swan Lake
Peter Ilyich Tchaikovsky, 1840-1893

Symphony No. 6
Ludwig van Beethoven, 1770-1827

Symphony No. 7
Ludwig van Beethoven, 1770-1827

Tetris Theme
Russian folk song, 19th century
Words: "Korobeiniki" Nikolai Nekrasov, 1821 -1878

The Banks Of The Ohio
Traditional ballad, 19th century

The Entertainer
Scott Joplin, 1868-1917

The First Noel
Words: Cornish. Edited by William Sandys, ca. 1823
Music: Traditional English Carol

The Muffin Man
Traditional nursery rhyme

This Old Man
Nursery rhyme, 1842
Music: unknown

Trumpet Concerto
Joseph Haydn, 1732-1809

Twinkle Twinkle Little Star
Words: Jane Taylor, 1783-1824
Music: anonymous pastoral song, 1740

Up on the Housetop
Words and music: Benjamin Hanby, ca. 1864

Water Music
Music: Georg Friedrich Handel, 1685-1759

We Wish You a Merry Christmas
Words and music: Arthur Warrell, 1935

Wedding March
Felix Mendelssohn Bartholdy, 1809-1847

Wellerman
Words: Unknown, 1860–1870
Music: Unknown, Sea song

William Tell Overture
Gioachino Rossini, 1792-1868

Yankee Doodle
American Traditioal

Notes and Rest

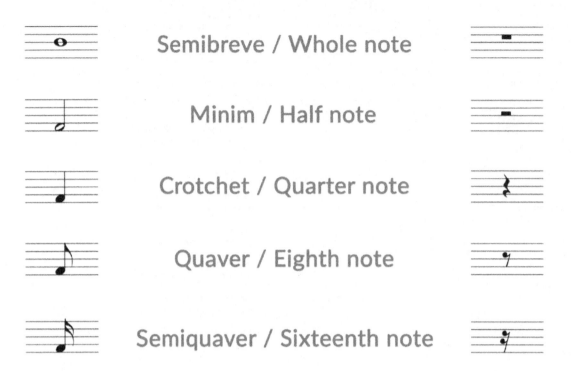

Semibreve / Whole note

Minim / Half note

Crotchet / Quarter note

Quaver / Eighth note

Semiquaver / Sixteenth note

Rhythm Tree

Length gets reduced by half for each step in the tree

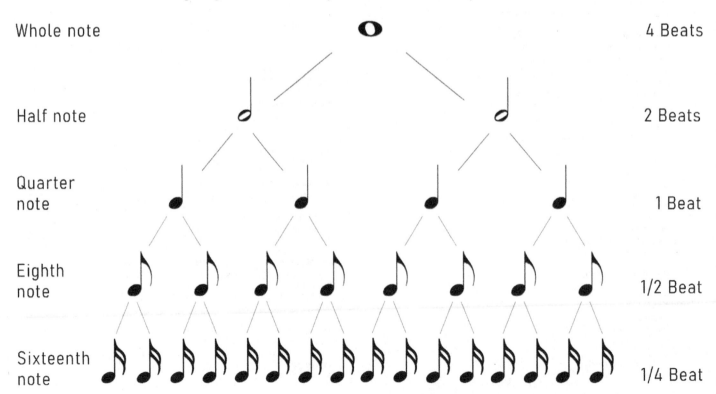

Whole note	4 Beats
Half note	2 Beats
Quarter note	1 Beat
Eighth note	1/2 Beat
Sixteenth note	1/4 Beat

Simple Time Signatures

Type of Beat	Duple Time	Triple Time	Quadruple Time
Crotchet Beat	$\frac{2}{4}$ ♩ ♩	$\frac{3}{4}$ ♩ ♩ ♩	$\frac{4}{4}$ ♩ ♩ ♩ ♩
Minim Beat	$\frac{2}{2}$ ♩ ♩	$\frac{3}{2}$ ♩ ♩ ♩	$\frac{4}{2}$ ♩ ♩ ♩ ♩
Quaver Beat	$\frac{2}{8}$ ♪ ♪	$\frac{3}{8}$ ♪ ♪ ♪	$\frac{4}{8}$ ♪ ♪ ♪ ♪

→ indicates number of beats per bar

→ indicates value of each beat

→ indicates there are 3 beats per bar

→ indicates each beat is a quarter note

→ indicates there are 4 beats per bar

→ indicates each beat is a quarter note

→ indicates there are 2 beats per bar

→ indicates each beat is a quarter note

Piano Notes Guide

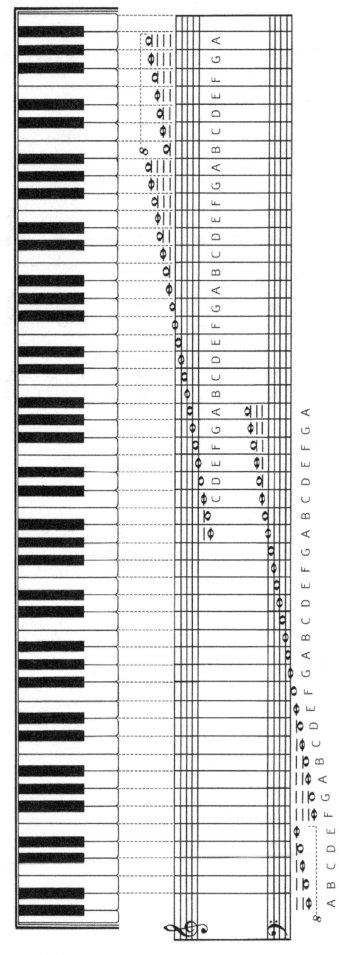

Circle of Fifths

Piano Chords 1

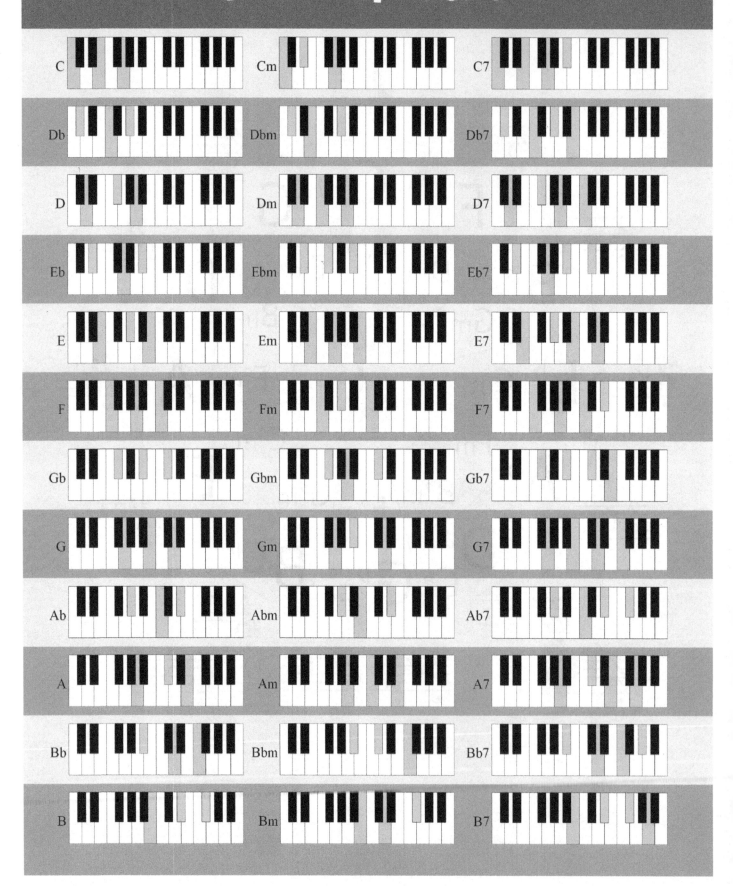

Piano Chords 2

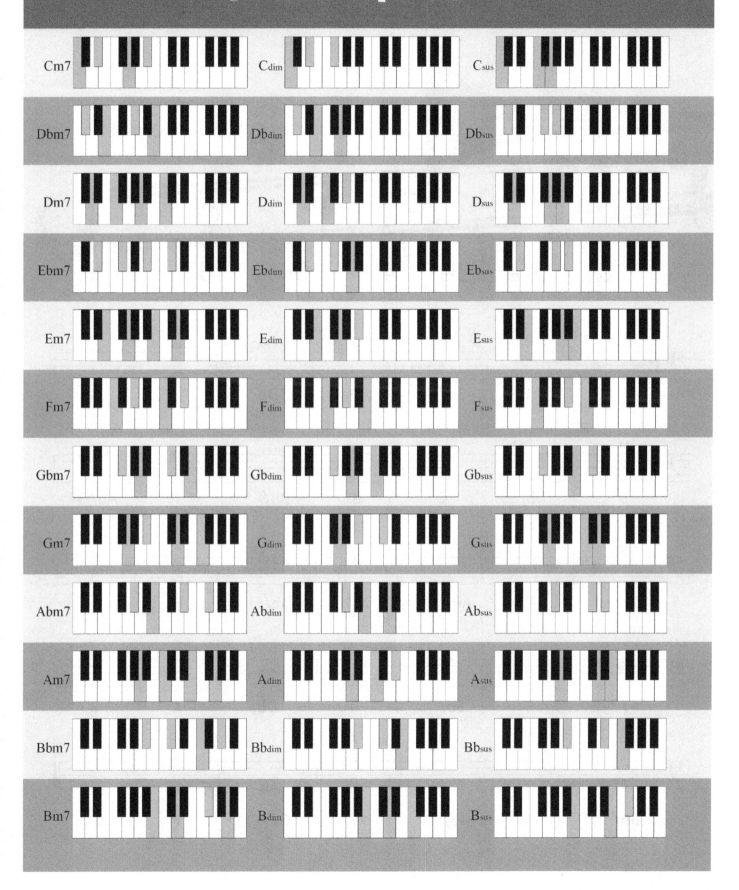

Trombone Slide Position Chart

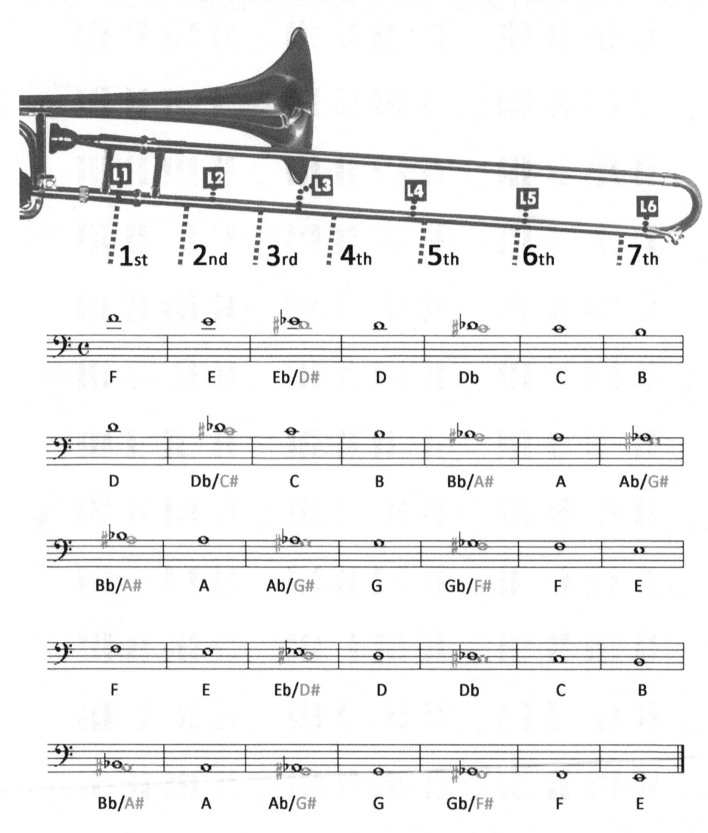

Made in United States
Orlando, FL
01 November 2024

53392690R00050